If It's To Be
(lessons in making sh*t happen)

©Copyright July 2018

James M. Lynch

For Rosie,
who always understood
what it meant to
never take 'no' for an
answer.

If It's To Be . . .

Welcome.

This book is for those solopreneurs (one-person shops), entrepreneurs, business owners, or for those in corporate jobs who want to dedicate themselves to getting results, getting things done, and going home at the end of a day thinking 'I did my best today' – and meaning it.

This is NOT a book about *positive thinking*. This isn't a HOW TO book about creating a business. This isn't even a book to convince you to invest in a new model, or franchise or GET RICH QUICK – though that last part would be nice.

This is a book about foundations, the basic contexts and mindsets that will help an entrepreneur survive the arduous task of making a business work. It is about building the 'muscle' that independence and tenacity use as foundations, and some tools and tricks to keep you going.

In my many years of working with businesses, corporate executives, and creative types, I've found that so many of them are being told what to think, how to do things and paying money they can't afford to be told to do exactly what they already know they should be doing. This is not so much *what to think* and it's certainly not a 'how to be an entrepreneur', but more a book about *how to think* in order to survive, in order to thrive.

Read it. Practice it. Build the muscle that you'll draw on to make your dreams come true. Today, as it turns out, is THE day you've been waiting for, so let's get started.

James M. Lynch
Your Chief Possibility Officer and
Vice President of Making Shit Happen

'Entrepreneur: someone who will work 60 hours a week to avoid working 40'.

Unknown

The (Make Believe) Land of 100% Responsibility

Let's start by tackling a tough but oh so important context.

This one is tough, but if you can 'go with it', suspend disbelief, and try it on, you'll see how amazingly freeing it can be.

Once you adjust to its logic you'll see that it can apply in every aspect of your life, giving back power where power has been lost.

Ok, so you're driving down the road and in your rearview mirror you notice a car coming up quick, driving erratically. 'What a jerk', you think, and continue on as the good and conscientious driver you are: staying within 5MPH of the speed limit, hands at '10 and 2' on the steering wheel, checking all mirrors regularly, etc. Before you know it, though, the jerk comes up beside you, swerves and sideswipes your car. You both pull over, the cops arrive, and it is clearly the other guy's fault. Right?

But you still have a dented car, right? *So, it being the other guy's fault helps you how*?

I came up with this context when I was sitting around a conference table, the boss asking AGAIN, who was responsible for this one piece of business that kept getting dropped.

Looking around the table I saw the 'not me' pose on the two people that I thought were the two most likely candidates to own this problem, but they both seemed to be staring intently at something about 15 inches from the table edge, midway between their two hands. It was as if they were unable to look up or look around.

And there was silence, lots of silence, especially when the boss asked again: 'Who is responsible for this?'

Not one to enjoy wasting time, to enjoy watching others squirm, or to see loose ends unravel, I raised my hand and said, 'I am. I don't have anything to say right now, but by next week's meeting I'll take this on and bring you results'.

The boss looked at me, surprised at first, then said, 'OK. Let's move on to the next item on the list'. We were able to finish the meeting and move on.

Later, the boss came to my office and said, "We all know that you weren't responsible for that issue, and yet you raised your hand. What's up?"

I told him that it didn't look like it was going to get handled any other way, that all that was important is that it got dealt with. I told him I didn't want to sit around and listen to excuses, blame or people pointing fingers. "Let me know if you need anything", he said, and he left.

It wasn't my responsibility, but I took it on, MADE BELIEVE it was my responsibility, solved the problem, and at the next meeting reported that all was good again.

The ability to affect a situation, whether it is your fault or not, to make it better, move the dial, get shit done, is part of the entrepreneur's mindset.

It doesn't matter who spilled the water on the café floor, it matters that no one slips and gets injured.

OK – let's take a breath. This is a tough one, and in your head, you're saying 'what the heck? This context means that you'll be blamed for everything. You'll be the victim. You'll be committing career suicide on a regular basis, and on and on. It seems over the top, right? It is. But it is meant as a POWER TOOL and is only there for those who are strong enough to wield it.

So how the 'heck' can you be 100% Responsible? What about the other guy? What about the person who doesn't show up, who doesn't respond, misses the deadline, breaks their promise, etc.

How can you be 100% responsible when so much depends on others? Exactly.

But you see, I don't care about anyone else. I only care about *you*. Your results are YOUR results. You have power in a situation or you don't. No, I'm not intentionally being flippant or vague with this concept. You just have to try it on.

Another example: Two weeks ago, I set an appointment with a potential client for Wednesday at 2PM, the coffee shop on White Street, just south of Black Avenue. We exchanged emails, had a nice phone chat, set up an appointment and then I sent them a calendar appointment with the date, place and time included. They accepted the appointment in their Outlook. It's on my calendar so I'm pretty sure it's on theirs.

Come Wednesday at 2PM and I'm at the coffee shop. I'm still there at 2:15. Alone. I'm finished my coffee at 2:30, and they're still not there. If they show up now, by the way, I can't spend more than a few minutes with them because I have another meeting at 3:30 in that same spot.

Obviously, it's their fault for not showing up.

I did everything I should for the appointment. They'll obviously have to apologize, or make an excuse, or try to reschedule. I was in the right, right?

I'm really only 50% responsible in this case, right, because I showed up, and they didn't. I couldn't go pick them up and drive them to the meeting, could I?

But I still have a wasted hour or more of my week, don't I?

So, in **The (Make Believe) Land of 100% Responsibility,** I want to know that every meeting takes place. I take 100% Responsibility for each meeting occurring, and never accept 50% as an option.

Remember it is called the 'make believe' land for a reason: because I'm not REALLY responsible for other people living up to their promises, but I ACT LIKE IT for the value it brings to me.

For instance, every Sunday I preview my week's schedule and I send reminders to all of the appointments that are not regularly set and recurring. I ask people to confirm with me. If I don't hear back from them in time I check in, again, the night before. I work to have as much advance notice of a change in my schedule as possible so that I have a chance to replace an appointment if I need to.

OK, one more. You have a friend you ask for help with a project. You explain you can't pay them much and that it's a favor you'll one day repay. You thank them profusely in advance.

It's really important that they help you and you know you can count on them because you've been there for them in the past. It's one hour of their life, but for you it's urgent and important. Then at 5 minutes before you expect them they text you that they have a conflict and are not going to be able to make it. Screw them, right?

So where does that leave you? It leaves you with no power in the matter, right? You are a victim here, and a righteous one at that.

In The (Make Believe) Land of 100% Responsibility you have LOTS of options. All of them lead to regaining power in the matter.

1. You realize that when you asked them for help you did it in a way that left them little room to say 'no'. They never were really committed to helping so when something came along to provide them with an excuse they felt OK with letting you down.
2. You could have set a backup for them. If it was REALLY urgent to have someone there to help, you want to have a plan 'B'.
3. You could have asked them 'no shit, no kidding' (see the NSNK chapter) and re-confirmed with them the day before.
4. What options could you come up with to prevent this from happening to you?

Now I realize that this is not how things SHOULD be, that no one is 100% Responsible for anyone else, and that this one may make you want to resist, but I ask that you *try this one out.*

> *The main use of The (Make Believe) Land of 100% Responsibility is used to take back power where power is lost. It is a way to let go of fault, blame, finger pointing and get to the point of ACTION.*

Note:
I'm not an idiot, really. If someone consistently lets me down, changes or misses appointments, I stop giving them the opportunity to disappoint me. As a coach, though, a lot of my work involves helping people keep their word, come to terms with being overscheduled, and other irresponsible behaviors. It's up to each of us to decide where our limit is and hold people accountable accordingly.

This context is not to make you a victim, but if you can handle it, it could just give you back power where power has been lost – as long as you realize that it is a CONTEXT, not reality, and that's why we use the words 'make believe'. Got it?

Note 2: A great side effect of this context is that you can completely re-wire your relationship to the words 'fault' and 'blame' to the point where they hold no consequence, no negative energy for you anymore. Now THAT would be great, right?

"Do, or not do. There is no try."

Yoda

"For all of the most important things, the timing always sucks. Waiting for a good time to quit your job? The stars will never align, and the traffic lights of life will never all be green at the same time. The universe doesn't conspire against you, but it doesn't go out of its way to line up the pins either. Conditions are never perfect. "Someday" is a disease that will take your dreams to the grave with you. Pro and con lists are just as bad. If it's important to you and you want to do it "eventually," just do it and correct course along the way."

Timothy Ferriss

Islands of Safety

Let's say you're at home on a dark, wintry night and the electricity goes out. You stumble around in the dark, 'where did I put that flashlight?' As you crack your shin on the coffee table for the second time you realize that you should pre-plan for just such an occasion. In the future you'll store a flashlight in a place where you'll be able to get your hands on it, even in the dark. Right?

That's the idea behind Islands of Safety, but it goes a bit further. An IOS can be a place, a person, a thing, some music, food, etc. But here's a warning: there are 'good' and 'bad' IOS, as in 'light/dark'.
- If you choose a 'dark IOS', you'll likely 'drown'.
- Choose a 'light' IOS, and you'll survive another day, rest, recharge, and go to the next 'port in a storm' as we cross the 'Inconsistent Sea' that is day to day life.

Think of the life of an entrepreneur as a journey across this Inconsistent Sea. You can swim or sail, but only for so long. When the weather gets bad, or the seas get choppy, you need to find solid ground.

But if you are already exhausted *before* you start looking for an oasis you may not make it there before you drown.

You need to set up Islands of Safety before you need them.

Good Islands of Safety are healthy. Before you go out on the 'Inconsistent Sea' you should 'chart' those healthy ports in the storm. They are where you'll retreat when things get rough. And things WILL get rough.

You'll see that in the life of an entrepreneur not every plan you make will work, that sometimes things go exactly the wrong way, that you may lose energy, motivation and the spirit to continue on moving towards your goal. It's important that in those times you don't give up the journey: just get to a place where you can recover, rest and get ready to keep going.

Sample 'good' IOS:

Nature. I know that walking in the woods, on the beach or just sitting in the back yard will help me collect my thoughts and put things into perspective. I can 'go there' to figure out a problem, or just to help me get over a disappointment.

Music. Do you have a piece of music that helps you concentrate while you're working?

People. We'll talk more about people in the next chapter, like having friends, mentors, peers, advisors, coaches, etc., so no need to say too much here. Just know who you can call when you're down or ready to sell yourself out or short.

Things. It's OK to keep awards, diplomas, and records of other milestones on the walls of your office. You're not 'showing off', or bragging, you're reminding yourself of past accomplishments to help you stick it through to your next accomplishment.

Or your IOS 'thing' could be a favorite picture or painting, a piece of driftwood, a stone, etc. It really doesn't matter what it is. If it gives you a 'positive vibe', if it keeps you moving forward, it is an IOS.

Bad Islands of Safety:

These are those things that offer some relief from pressure, but that actually leave you drained and weaker. They offer you a break, a little respite for a while, but in the long run, you're better off without them.

I know you can figure these out: alcohol (too much), food (too much), sex (without meaning), and all of those 'numbing' behaviors that give us a little break, but no real relief.

I'm not going to 'beat you up' about the bad ones, the 'dark' side, I'm aware that sometimes people go there. Just don't go there too often and avoid them when you can.

Do you know where your 'flashlights' are right now?

Coaches All Around You

We're still in preparation for the entrepreneur's journey and we're identifying the tools and resources we need to be 'set' for fulfilling our commitments.

Being a coach myself it may seem self-serving to tell you that you'll do better if you have a coach, but I am duty bound to tell you the truth. The good news is that there are always plenty of supporters around you.

Coaches – these are the people who inspire and motivate you. They don't push you out of the way, take over, and do it for you. (When was the last time you saw a football coach remove a quarterback from the field and then take their place?)

These are the people who say, 'you can do it', who might even offer a tool for you to use to figure something out or create a strategy. They won't let you make excuses for real results. They will hold you accountable, hold your feet to the fire, and you will perform better because of them.

Consultants – these are the people who can give advice because they've been there, but more importantly they can take on a project on your behalf and deliver results. They have specialized knowledge of all or part of your industry and will study your problem and offer a solution. They take action and solve things on request. They work for you, with you, and move an issue forward.

Advisors/Connectors – these are people who know people. Say you're in need of an accountant, bookkeeper, or other professional service that it makes more sense to outsource than do on your own. They offer their thoughts, inspiration, but don't tell you what you HAVE to do. A good advisor is there for whatever the situation is and invested in your success.

Mentors – these are the people who have the benefit of experience and are there to help you grow.

Traditionally they are older, experienced and their success is measured by your growth and success. What's important with a mentor, especially in a corporate environment, is that there's an agreement in place, with a definition of what the relationship will look like, and some boundaries. A mentor is not a guru.

Gurus – are mostly to be avoided. Not all gurus are harmful, true, but most – especially self-appointed ones - are a waste of time at least. These are the people who advertise on social media that they've got a system that will give you an endless supply of clients, a perpetual sales funnel, and show you how to 'make money while you sleep', etc.

Their free seminar/webinar is a come-on to get you to buy something. Even if their 'guaranteed model' works, if they do have value, your time is better spent focusing on marketing, delivering and honing your own process and business model. (Then *you* can hold a 'how to seminar' to help people make money while they sleep).

The lesson here is that often entrepreneurs want to do it all by themselves. 'Natural entrepreneurs' and solo-preneurs are often so independent that they can have an 'automatic no' ready for any situation. The problem is that sometimes you miss a really good opportunity because you obsessively want to do it 'on your own'.

> *In order to succeed as an entrepreneur one skill you'll have to sharpen is listening.*

It's better to 'hear' than just to listen. And the answer to people's suggestions when they're trying to help you is 'thank you'. It's a 'yes' in the way that it's a statement of 'I hear you', but it is not a 'yes' in the way of 'I'll do that'.

> *You have to weigh the input with the consequences and see what comes of it. There's never a guarantee either way.*

To be a winning entrepreneur I suggest you occasionally take stock to make sure you have an adequate supply of the following: Inspiration, Motivation, Education and Fun. These are all things that the 'coaches' all around you can provide.

The Wrong Coach

Cheryl was surprised by a knocking sound on her second-story office window – *from the outside*. When she pulled open the blinds her friend, Alice, was hovering in the air, flapping her wings in flight.

Throwing open the window she asked: 'What are you doing, Alice?'

'I'm flying', said Alice. 'Isn't it great?'

'But Alice' she said, 'People can't fly. It's physically impossible'.

'It is?' Asked Alice, her spirits beginning to sag.

'Of course, silly Alice, it's just not possible.'

'Oh', said Alice. Then she stopped flapping her arms and fell to the ground. She never tried to fly again.

Be careful with whom you share your dreams.

Everything that follows the word 'because' is a lie.

Think about it. This is sometimes the most controversial statement I make. People push back that sometimes things actually do happen that weren't expected, that there are often 'good' reasons why things break down, etc. *(If you're stuck: Go back to the chapter on The (Make Believe) Land of 100% Responsibility, then read on.)*

Let's say that you fail to deliver a client's merchandise on time 'because' your driver didn't show up for work. Does that make the merchandise magically show up at the customer's office?

> What have you got the most of:
> results, or reasons?

Does the client CARE why it isn't there, or just that they counted on you and your disappointed them and the consequences to their business? So, the 'because' is just a waste of time.

Explaining why something didn't happen is not helpful in most cases because nothing changes because of it. So why waste time saying 'because' of 'so and so' . . .

This is NOT as narrow a definition as the title of this chapter implies, of course, as there can always be a breakdown and sometimes the only way to save a situation is to offer an excuse, but it is the principal of results vs. reasons we want to emphasize.

If you don't do what you said you would do by when you said you would do it, you're out of integrity. Get back into integrity by admitting you're out of it, recommitting, then make it happen.

If it happens again, then you're really not committed to making it happen and you are avoiding some basic breakdown in your process, organization or on your team.

Try not to say 'because' and instead 'be the cause' of things happening.

Some people may *want* an excuse, sometimes you need to share one to save the situation and mollify someone else, but most times it just weakens your power and puts you at the mercy of circumstance.

So, what we're talking about is not the literal interpretation of an intentionally provocative statement. We're talking about adopting the most powerful mindset, of 'girding your loins' as an entrepreneur, and being fully 'the cause'.

Make it happen.

FREDA

I met Freda in a Communications Course for which I was a volunteer coach. One day she told me her story.

She was in her mid-fifties and a single mom when the owners of the garden tool company she worked for announced to the team that 'it was over'. With no advance notice, no strategy for the employees' future, the owners just closed up shop and told everyone 'good bye'.

A single mom with a young daughter to care for, she decided to contact her clients and ask them if they'd buy directly from her. Then she called the factory in Japan and asked them if they'd extend her credit until she could build up the business a bit. She convinced them that taking a risk was better than no business at all.

The next few years were very hard for Freda, but she persevered and eventually had a team of people working under her. Soon her new company was doing better than the one she'd been let go from. It was at this point she decided to take some classes in 'how to' run a business. She contacted a local women in business group and signed up for classes in entrepreneurship, starting a business, keeping books, marketing plans, etc.

What she learned from the courses, she said, was that starting a business is really hard. In fact, she said, if she had taken the courses *before* she started her business, she wouldn't have done it. She was very glad she created the business before someone told her how hard it would be.

She just made it happen, one step at a time.

OK – One more thing about cause, reason, etc. Here's a useful principal to know.

Occam's Razor – after William of Ockham, friar, philosopher and theologian, from the late 13th, early 14th century, this principal says 'the simpler the explanation the better' or the solution with the fewest assumptions, the shortest distance between what was happening and what might be the cause, was the best.

What it means to you. If you're selling something online and you're getting great 'hits' to your website, but 'dwell time' is short, or people are leaving your website quickly, then it's not that people have short attention spans, or that

> "Whenever possible, substitute constructions out of known entities for inferences to unknown entities."
>
> Bertrand Russell

you're getting a bunch of 'I'm just looking' types, it's because your website isn't drawing them in.

If you run a restaurant and business is bad it's usually food quality or service that's turning them off. Don't buy a fancy espresso machine or bring in fifty flavors of gelato (or whatever is IN lately). Make the answer simple.

The modern variation of this is: 'If it looks like a duck, walks like a duck, quacks like a duck, it's probably a duck.'

Razor in this case does not exactly mean a sharp-edged knife used by hipsters to shave *around* their bushy beards, but the *principal* used to 'shave away' unnecessary thought.

A must-see scene is in the movie Gattaca. Vincent and his brother are swimming across the lake. His brother has asked him how he has been fooling so many people for so long. As they swim across the lake the brother says, 'I can't go on, let's go back'. Vincent says, 'That's how I did it. I'm already past the point that I could make it back. I HAVE to go ahead.'

Plateaus

What happens when you've been working really hard, things are going pretty well, and then you hit a 'plateau' where nothing new is happening? Results are stagnant, or worse yet, you begin to slide backwards.

I'm going to use three sources to discuss this. But first let's say unless you're a wunderkind with a new tech advance that's going to revolutionize an industry you have to expect a slump from time to time. Recognizing that you're in a slump and not freaking out or taking extreme measures is important.

So first let's talk about **Mastery: The Keys to Success and Long-Term Fulfillment**, by George Leonard. In the book, which I will not do a good service to in summing it up here (I recommend buying a copy right now), Leonard uses the lessons he's learned from martial arts to show us the 'Mastery Curve'.

Breakthroughs are the quick, short-lived results of many hours of practice. You spend more time on the 'plateau' than you do on the 'up arrow', so be patient and do the everyday practices that eventually produce a breakthrough. If you're living for the 'big deal', the high of a great event, then you're setting your expectations up for a fail.

Seth Godin, in **The Dip** warns you that every business should expect a 'slump' where they feel stuck in a rut, the 'dip', when things get really hard and it's all effort. No fun. He warns that you should know if you're in a slump that you can get out of or a Cul-de-Sac with no place to go.

If you're a restaurateur, for instance, how far will you dip into your savings, run up your credit card, exhaust your bank loan and/or borrow from your kid's college fund before you say 'enough'?

So, while Leonard advises you to keep practicing, keep doing the small things that create the big results, Godin says know when to quit and get out before it's too late. Then start the next thing. I'll include a reading list in the back of the book, but these two are worth investing in right away.

What should you, the solo-preneur/entrepreneur be thinking? First of all, plan for the worst and keep plenty of cash on hand. That's rule #1, #2, #3 (and probably #4-#10). Keep cash on hand and don't overspend.

If throwing money at a problem makes it go away it's not really a problem, and we all have to realize that things happen in their own time sometimes, no matter how hard we try and force them.

We need to be able to see the forest for the trees, make good decisions and decide when we are just down, or when we're out.

"When everything seems to be going against you, remember that the airplane takes off against the wind, not with it."

Henry Ford

NO Thinking in Bed

'Objects at rest tend to stay at rest'. Or more likely in the entrepreneur's case: at 'rest-less'.

I don't know about you, but one of my most vulnerable times for negative self-talk is when I'm in bed.

Whether I'm worried about something in particular, something specific that wakes me up in the middle of the night, or those moments when I first wake up when I lay there thinking about the mountain of things I need to do.

Sometimes I just want to pull the covers over my head and stay hidden from the world. But that never works, does it?

There's an acronym I remember, and I think there's another half of it that I've forgotten, but it reminds people of what conditions we should avoid making decisions or negotiating with others from. HALT stands for hungry, angry, lonely or tired.

If these conditions exist, the likelihood of a positive outcome is lessened. So, stop thinking and feeling. OK?

Really. Thinking and feeling just mess things up.

I like it when my clients say to me 'I hear your voice in my head, James, telling me . . .' When they say that it means my message is getting through and new habits are developing. OK, I know you can't stop either thinking or feeling, but you can choose what you do because of them – or not.

The message I want YOU to hear in the back of your head is this: "We are not our thoughts. We are not our feelings. We are the committed actions we take to realize our promises".

Lying in bed in the morning our thoughts and feelings begin to fight with our true commitment. I say 'true' commitment, because you can also be committed to comfort, sameness, ease, and some negative or dark beliefs. It's easier to be convinced that we don't really need to do all we said we'd do, that it would be better for us in the long run to roll over and get a little more sleep, that we can skip that one meeting *because* . . . (Everything that follows the word 'because' is a lie, remember?).

Get in the habit of taking care of yourself. Eat right and healthily – entrepreneurs are playing a long-term game and solopreneurs can't call in sick to anyone (other than themselves).

Learn to process anger through any process that works for you. Have your 'Islands of Safety' and identify the coaches all around you so that you know whom to reach out to when you feel all alone. Get to bed early and manage your sleep.

There will always be more to do, but you'll do more when you've taken time to reenergize and refresh.

When the alarm goes off, whether it's 4AM or 6AM, whether it's a beautiful summer day or a blustery, snowy -20 degrees, jump out of bed and get started.

If you need to, imagine a hand reaching down from above, grabbing you by the collar and hauling your butt out of bed – whatever it takes – just don't lay there and think negative thoughts. It's a waste of time.

"To hell with circumstances. I create opportunities."

Bruce Lee

Love the Solution More Than the Problem

If you were to listen to people at parties, on grocery lines, family events, etc., it seems that one of the most common uses for talk is to *complain*.

People love to talk about what's wrong and its usually some anonymous cabal in charge – 'they'. You know what 'they say', or 'No use trying, the deck is stacked against us', 'The more things change, the more they remain the same', and lots of other victim/problem talk.

It drives me crazy, yes, I'm venting, when people say they can't do something because first s*omething else* has to happen and *that* depends on something else. 'I can't lose weight because I'm taking this medication for my condition, and the pills make me retain water and drain my energy . . .' It's a vicious cycle of not getting anywhere.

And it doesn't work when people just SAY 'let's focus on the solution, not the problem'. They mostly tend to just re-state the problem and come away with a plan that depends on something else, someone else, or is a deferred 'if only', 'if all goes well', 'as long as they do X', etc. None of which is really a plan but a gaping maw of a back door for NOT getting anywhere.

Solution focus is not about what did or didn't work before. 'We tried that a few years ago, it didn't work . . .' (I'll shoot the next person who says that to me – with a water gun. Don't worry, I'm sane).

Solution focus is to start by saying 'what would happen if we . . .', then breaking the process down into the smallest possible steps that create anything even resembling progress.

Solution focus means going slow, getting a 1% advance in the situation or circumstance, so that you move further and further away from the 'stuck' state of problem-focused thinking.

Here's a tool to use for any issue. It's so simple it has only ONE real rule and that is to start with the SIMPLEST issue to fix. (No kidding, I got an email from someone saying it wasn't working for him. I asked, 'which item did you start with' and he said, 'the most important one'. "In other words, the hardest?" I asked. "Yes, it's the most important, too". "Did you not hear me say, 'start with the SIMPLEST?" "Yes, but . . .")

See Next Page

The Working/Not Working 'Tree'.

Draw a two-column list and label the left side 'Working' and the Right 'Not Working' (See Next Page)

Then pick a problem you're having and write down at least 3 items on each side. Most people fill up the 'Not Working' side pretty well; but you have to have at least 3 'Working' items too.

Next take the SIMPLEST, easiest item from the Not Working side of the list and create an 'action list' of things that would move that simplest of all problems to the other side. Once the item has the action list MOVE it to the 'Working' side. Get it done and then go back to the next SIMPLE issue. This is about 'building muscle', like going to a gym and starting with the lightest weights first, then building up to the heavier weights.

Use this tool often as the process of writing down and listing issues is a way to get your brain figuring out a solution. Even just writing down the issues and coming back to them at a later time works – your brain will be problem solving in its 'dark recesses' until you're ready to get to work.

Working	Not Working

Action List

1.
2.
3.
4.
5.

Family – Cat's in the Cradle

'Cat's in the Cradle' by folk singer Harry Chapin, is the story of a boy asking his dad 'when you coming home?' and the dad making excuses for not being there until, as you might imagine, it's the retired father in the same spot, asking his son 'do you have time for me'? Well, what business is worth losing your family for?

This section of the book is about keeping the business alive, but without paying too high a price for the success you seek. It's about work/life balance, if you want to call it that, or emotional health, prioritization, honoring the family – whatever works for you – and it relates back to 'Islands of Safety'. If you're going to skip a chapter, don't skip this one.

Rituals are the 'non-negotiables' that you're going to keep up no matter what happens. They are rocks in the river that don't change with the ebb and flow.

Spiritual Services – If you don't have one now, develop some sort of spiritual life. Closing down business for 24 hours once a week will give you time to recoup, clear your brain, recharge and (re)gain perspective. If you're an online business, there are plenty of tools to implement to keep things going while you're away. If you're a brick and mortar operation, then shutting down for one day will just be the way you define yourself to your customers and audience. That's important, to define yourself to your customers and not let them define you.

Meditation - If you're not part of any religious organization, you still owe yourself a day a week to take a break. Short of that, a regular practice of meditation can give you exponential rewards. Think about it as 'slowing down' and 'changing the oil' mentally so that your gears don't grind themselves to ruin.

Journaling – Keeping track of what you're experiencing on a day to day basis can help you make better decisions and better recognize even the small accomplishments of each day. Consider setting a quick goal for the day and going after it. It could be some productivity amount or just a 'way of being', like how you'll treat people. At the end of the day, consider 'what did I learn?'

Family time – in my family we 'religiously' have dinner together every Friday night. We have a family brunch on Sundays and get together Sunday night for pizza and a movie. The rest of the week we try, with sports, clubs, work, friends, to have dinner as a family as often as possible, but the Friday and Sunday rituals are non-negotiable. They are the rocks.

Self-Care – Rituals that are helpful are the ones that help us 'stay sane', as I wrote before. If you're going to run a business you need to be in the *space* to make healthy decisions, work long hours, and maintain a positive attitude. You can't just count on your brain, you need to take care of your body. A healthy approach to eating is the best start you can make. You put in the right kind of fuel, the energy and production will follow.

Also, we store our emotions, upsets and fears in our bodies, tensing and suppressing, getting tighter and tighter, more rigid and immovable with each day. It's important that you find a way to move your body. Lifting weights, an early AM run, yoga, cycling to and from work, all are ways to maintain balance and health. Don't underestimate the value of a good workout to help you stay on track with your other goals.

True Story

During one particularly busy time I told my daughter that I was sorry for being so preoccupied recently. I explained that I was in the middle of a big project but that I'd be more available in a short time. She told me it was 'no problem', and that it was OK that I was so busy.

I wondered if she meant that it didn't matter to her if I was around or not, but what she meant, as it turns out, is that she could recognize when I was 'up to something' and be patient. She knows how important my family is to me and that she could trust me to finish things and then be available again.

It wasn't that she didn't care if I was around, it's that she knew from experience that I'd do the right thing. It was a fortifying vote of confidence.

F_____ Your Spouse

Wait a moment, you don't think I mean, uh, no, I mean FORGIVE your spouse. They'll be the ones who give you feedback, tell you when you're overdoing it, out of line, out of balance, and when to slow down. They may even be your literal partners in making things happen, so make sure you keep a LARGE EMOTIONAL CASH RESERVE FOR YOUR SPOUSE. If they ask, are doubtful, are questioning, don't take it personally. Let them be the mirror that accurately, even painfully, reflects you as you are at that time. Listen, weigh, respond, and keep your vision for your entrepreneurship in perspective.

Another reason you may need to forgive them is that they can sometimes be the mirror for our own feelings of fear and inadequacy if things are not going well. The term is 'projection' and, even if they're quiet, or may just mention an overdue bill, etc., unless they are LITERALLY complaining, don't let yourself put your own experience onto what they HAVEN'T EVEN SAID.

If you're not getting what I am writing here, then put it aside for now. Make an appointment with yourself to check back in though, at a later time. This one is VERY important. Don't lose your 'life partner' over a business. YOU are responsible, remember, and they can support you, but they can't absorb blame if you want to play that game and, 'there's no cheese down that tunnel'.

"Twenty years from now, you will be more disappointed by the things that you didn't do than by the ones you did do, so throw off the bowlines, sail away from safe harbor, catch the trade winds in your sails. Explore, Dream, Discover."

Mark Twain

Feedback

It's important that you learn how to receive feedback. It can be feedback about poor results for sales, it can be a pattern of behavior that you're developing, it can just be that you're in danger of making a bad decision. Look back to the chapter 'Coaches All Around You' for more on input from others. But this section is a bit briefer, about tools and specifics.

There are basically 5 ways we can handle feedback and four of them account for about ninety-five percent of all reactions.

Defend – we'll make excuses for what's going on. We'll say it wasn't our fault and resist the input we're getting.

Deflect – we're going to divert anything that comes at us, avoiding 'getting anything on us'. We'll be the target of feedback and we'll try to change the topic, bring up someone or something else, compare or complain. 'So-what if I am charging more for the same thing. What do you think Nordstrom's does?'

Deny – 'Nope. No. Didn't happen'. This is a direct argument against what's happening, a lie sometimes, or sometimes we want something to be true so badly that we make it true in our minds, but it doesn't change anything. The longest river in the world and the surest way to lose track of reality – Denial (da Nile? Hah, hah.)

Attack – 'I know you are, but what am I?' That's when you turn everything around on the person who is offering you feedback and make it about them. It's clever if it works because if the other person feels attacked they automatically go into the 'Defend, Deflect, Deny, and maybe Attack back' and it becomes a cycle.

Oh yes, one other option. I said FIVE, right? Only this one is so rarely used it's easy to forget. And it's a shame, because this is the one with the most value.

Accept – Yes, that's right, you can accept feedback and just say 'thank you'. You can consider the input without committing to taking action by the way, as accepting info, whether or not you actually act on it or not. You can even get feedback, good or bad AND take action on it. It's actually considered 'gracious' to be open and accepting of input – as in the similar root to 'grateful'.

What ARE You Committed To?

So, you *say* you're committed to your business success, and that looks like a million dollars in sales, or maybe certain behaviors, like spending an hour a day on marketing, etc. Let's see how this is working out.

It's time for another T-chart. Draw a line down the center of a blank page, then a line across the top, so that you have something that looks very much like the 'Working/Not Working' list. Now on the top left write 'Committed To' and on the top right, add 'Actual/Showing Up'.

Now write what you say you are committed to on the right side. Like '$1 mil in gross sales', or '25 customer calls a week', one hour of social media a day', etc. You can even add personal and health items like: weigh 180 lbs., exercise 5x a week, no weekday dessert, etc.

On the left side, write what is actual and showing up for each of those items. So, if you're looking for $1 mil in gross sales and you're actually getting $100k; or next to '25 customer calls a week' you write that you're actually only making 15; or your committed to weighing 180 lbs. and actually weigh 199 lbs., etc. Make the list about different commitments across all areas of your life.

Now the next part of this exercise is a 'surprise', so in case you're the type who reads ahead, I'm going to skip a half a page. Finish your list and don't turn the page until you have at least 10 items with both sides filled out.

Go ahead. I'll wait.

What ARE You Committed To, Part 2

Now follow the instructions very carefully for this next part.

On the top left, cross out 'Committed To'. Then, on the right side, cross out the 'Actual/Showing Up' title. THEN, on the top right side, re-write the words 'Committed To'. Pause.

If you've done this correctly, the right side will now be titled 'Committed To'. What do you think of that?

You should be thinking that what is ACTUALLY SHOWING UP is what you're REALLY committed to. After all, that's what you're producing, right? Unless someone's putting a gun to your head you're the one responsible for the results, or lack of them. And if you're REALLY committed to something, it will begin showing up in the 'results' column.

It's important that you don't use this tool to beat yourself up or stop here by being discouraged. It's not about that: it's about getting real, taking stock, and deciding if that's good enough for you or not.

The next step COULD be creating an action plan that's more realistic, that's something that you CAN accomplish, and getting to it. Get in 'relation' to your word, and live as if you say it, it's going to happen. Which leads to one of my principles that might help you create more wins: NSNK.

NSNK and the Tough Boss

When I was the General Manager of a sales and recruiting organization, I tried to get results through my top people. I gave them expectations and then the responsibility to get results from their own teams. We had daytime teams and, since we were in the Midwest and dealt with the west coast, we had evening shift teams. They all had specific goals and we checked them constantly.

If a team was NOT hitting their goals over time their biggest fear is that they knew I would take the team over until it turned around. Some of the people knew what it was like to be managed directly by me; some didn't have firsthand experience. So, when a team fell behind for too long and needed remedial action, they awaited the summons to the training room where they'd meet me. Fear and doubt were on their faces and their team leaders would usher them in as if they were about to 'get it'.

Here's what I did: I would ask each individual salesperson/recruiter what they needed to do to get the results they wanted. I recorded what actions they would commit to taking within the next week. Then I released them. Most of the time they would leave the room with a look of relief, knowing they didn't have to meet with me for a week.

A week later I would call them back to the training room. They'd come in with a more relaxed manner because the last meeting was non-threatening: no yelling, no 'coffee is for closers' speech. But those who had worked with me before knew that the hard work was about to start.

I would go around the room and ask: 'did you do what you said you would do. Yes or no?' This is where it got interesting, and tough.

They were not allowed to add anything other than those two words: yes or no. If they *had* done what they said they would, they were comfortable saying 'yes'.

If they hadn't done what they said, most of them hadn't by the way, they tended to 'explain' why. The hard part was that they couldn't get used to just saying 'no' without an explanation.

It took a long time and plenty of repeating, just say 'yes or no' until they finally would get it, but often you could see them nearly worn out. In fact, I never 'made them wrong' or commented on their 'no': I just catalogued it.

Then we'd go through the process again. 'What will you do by one week from today that will get you the results you want to achieve?' Again, we recorded what they committed to with attention to details: how many, by when. Then we released them again to get to work.

After a few weeks of this, those that were doing what they said they would, would start getting results. If they were doing what they said they needed to and weren't getting results, they either needed to step it up, or they needed remedial support (or possibly they just didn't have what it took to succeed).

Those that said 'no' each week realized that they were bullshitting not only us, but themselves. Again, if there were obstacles, we'd support them. If they just couldn't handle the pressure, do the right thing, etc., that became obvious and we took appropriate action.

What they got from me was the distinction 'no shit, no kidding', or NSNK. They learned that not getting results combined with a good excuse was still 'not getting results'. Try explaining to the check in desk at the airport why you're late *after* the plane has already taken off.

They got the value of committing to something and actually doing it or knowing the difference when they fell short. It wasn't about beating them up or making them feel 'wrong', though some people had a harder time than others understanding the 'black/white' quality of the exercise.

So, when someone makes you a promise, and you want to rely on it, ask them if it is a NSNK promise, or a 'if all goes well . . .', or 'unless something happens . . .', or if they really mean 'if I'm not distracted by something else . . . '

If you're going to be a successful entrepreneur, find out who in your life is a NSNK type and find a way to work with them more often. Those people who don't know the difference between a promise and an excuse are always going to be there. Find a way to deal with their confusion.

And do your best to live your life with a NSNK attitude. It will attract the right business and people to you in the long run.

(Thank you to Andrea, Bill, Esra, Hank, Linda, Mary, Tom and the others who became my NSNK team and the model of success for others that followed them)

The Invisible Hand or 'Start With Why', and a Shameless Riff on the Two

I was born in New York City, moved to Florida for my teens and early twenties, then back to NYC for a few years. While I was there I worked about 4 different jobs at the same time, sometimes working 24 hours straight. I was in my mid-twenties, so I could do that. And I liked the money.

Being up in the middle of the night in the 'city that never sleeps' I was amazed at how things got done. For instance, one job I had was catering video production shoots, like commercials, music videos, etc., and I had to be at the shop around 4 AM. On the way to work I'd see rock stars getting out of limos and going into late night clubs, others dragging home from later night jobs or partying. I'd see the owners and workers of breakfast spots and newspapers kiosks setting up for the day. And one of the great pleasures was to be the first one at H&H Bagels on the upper West Side, getting supplies for the catering job, and sampling the fresh, hot bagels they'd bagged for us.

At that time, I thought of something called 'The Invisible Hand' as those people who worked while I slept, who drove the trucks, stocked the shelves and made sure that the corner deli always had fresh supplies.

I didn't wonder about how it got done, because I saw the 'elves' at work all night long, driving, baking, delivering, sweeping the streets and I had nothing but respect for the people who did the work – whether they were the employee or the owner. Ask a baker what he or she is doing at 2AM while you're sleeping!

Then I found out that Adam Smith, around late 18th Century, just about when America was fighting for its political and financial freedom, was describing an 'invisible hand' that guided a free economy.

His theory, with inexact brevity, is that starting a business or selling a product for self-gain or totally selfish aims can't but help to benefit the society in general – unintended consequences. It also says that prices will re-set and adjust according to circumstances and competition.

I'm not here to argue the free market or regulation, but I mention this because you can only charge what you can charge in correlation to other products and competitors. If you think you'll charge a high fee, make a million and your product or service is so great that the public will beat a path to your door . . . Unlikely. And as soon as you're open to the public someone will knock you off, copy or undersell you. It's called 'making a buck'.

Now here's where 'Start With Why' comes in. In one of the most popular TED talks of all time Simon Sinek explains this in about fifteen minutes. Look it up. Watch it. (In fact, watch TED talks often and make them an 'Island of Safety' to inspire you when you're feeling stuck). To save time though, I'll explain it briefly.

If you are in touch with your WHY, the reason you're in business, the reason your product helps people, you'll be more motivated than if you sell the 'what'. Which statement is more enrolling: 'We sell really great refrigerators' or 'We bring good things to life'?

WHY would you put your time, your money, your life into a product? How will it benefit the world? What will it do for people?

Do you know someone who is a police officer? Do people get involved and ask about their jobs if they describe themselves as 'just a cop'? How about someone who says 'I make it possible for people to sleep at night and feel safe in their beds'? Now that would prompt you to say 'tell me more', wouldn't it?

Can you imagine yourself 'resupplying the city' as I originally understood the principal, as you contribute to the good of all, to the rest of society?

Can you do that knowing that others will try to beat you, take your business, under-sell you, and it's not because they're 'bad'?

Can you put up with government input, interference, taxes and regulation as an expected part of success?

Is your WHY you do this a big enough umbrella to shelter it all when it rains or pours?

                            Think about it before you commit

Tools and Resources: Decision Making

With some of these resources I'm opening my 'bag of tricks' or showing you 'behind the Wizard's curtain". If you read and research these resources, you will have more tools at your disposal. Remember, I'm here to help YOU win!

Best/Worst That Can Happen – If you have time, just kidding: whether you have time or not you need to learn how to make a good decision.

You can't just say 'I've got a good track record', as thinking and deciding are processes and you can always improve them. But before I tell you about the resources, let me introduce a tool for you to use.

When you're making a big decision or trying to solve a big problem, take it to the 'think tank'. Trying to consider things from as neutral a position as possible do this writing exercise.

Write down, 'If I do this, the worst thing that could happen is . . .' and then fill out at least three, hopefully more, possible outcomes. Be as brutally honest and 'negative' as you can. *Try to hurt your own feelings*!

Now do the exercise again with the starting phrase, 'If I do this, the best that could happen is . . .' Now do the same as above: create at least three, hopefully more, scenarios that fit the statement. Be as optimistic and positive as you can.

Review all of the statements. In fact, if you can do this with a trusted friend or advisor it works best.

Then ask yourself: are you ready for the worst that could happen as a consequence? If you were to choose the best that could happen, what concrete and real steps would you take (see The (Make Believe) Land of 100% Responsibility) to make sure that outcome came true? Will the ROI, return on investment, be worth your time, energy and financial commitment?

Do this exercise often but do it on paper. A lot of people do this in their heads constantly, some to the point that it makes them a bit crazy but doing it with an actual scratch pad makes all the difference in results.

OK, now to the Big Thinkers I mentioned at the start of this section. One of the aims of this book is to offer coaching services and resources that you may not be able to afford on your own.

1. Daniel Kahneman is a Nobel Prize winning economist who wrote **'Thinking, Fast and Slow '**. Through a series of experiments, he developed the 'prospect theory' that mirrors more closely how people *actually* make decisions, as opposed to how they *should* make decisions. With his partner, Amos Tversky, they outlined some "systematic

errors in the thinking of normal people". So, if you're going to be selling services or products to 'normal' people, read their book.

2. **Decisive**, by Chip and Dan Heath, is another good source for making better decisions. I could just say 'read everything these brothers write' and I would be giving you good advice, but to help you move faster, start here. They offer the acronym WRAP to help you remember their process.

- Widen your options,
- Reality-test your assumptions
- Attain distance before deciding
- Prepare to be wrong.

I can't share much more of their process without having to ask their permission to use their materials, but the steps are pretty self-explanatory, right?

According to them (and I agree) human beings are flawed machines operating from a series of biases, so we're constantly making and repeating mistakes.

Because: *we don't think so well.* Go figure.

Random Bits of Do/Don't Do

Choice – Can you adapt the mindset that it's all 'choice'? You choose to win or lose. You choose to make it hard or easy. You visit 'The (Make Believe) Land of 100% Responsibility' every day you go to work and say 'no' to being a victim. EVER.

> **"Do what you can, with what you have, where you are"**
> Theodore Roosevelt

If you go down the road of entrepreneurship you will get a lot of grief, stress, pain, stress, hard work – did I mention stress? – but it can be so rewarding that it is, in the end, all worth it.

Waiting for the right time. I tell my clients that if they're waiting for things to be 'just right', for the perfect alignment of the stars, etc., that the next 'waiting' they'll be doing is as *wait staff* telling people about today's specials.

If you wait for perfect, you'll miss 'good'. You'll miss 'done'. Stop waiting for others to do anything, for the market to be perfect, for your moon to be in Saturn, and get your ass moving. Don't be stupid, yes, but don't wait so long that your moment passes.

Judging others – I wear a red string around my left wrist to remind me that every time I judge others, I am reflecting that judgment back on myself. If we don't check ourselves on this topic we'll spend our lives consistently labeling people 'good' or 'bad' and filing them away accordingly. What a lot of time and energy on such a foolish mindset!

When you do business with people you are helping them, not judging them (unless that is a part of what your concept is), and it's best to open up to a wider view of the world where you realize that not everyone is going to be like you or share your values.

That doesn't mean you accept obviously 'bad' behavior, but it does mean giving everyone the benefit of a doubt (BOD).

Treat each person with trust and care. You will find that is it better to be vulnerable and suffer a few losses than to be suspicious and miss untold number of opportunities.

There will be people you just can't abide – true – but what do you want: them to die so you won't have to practice patience? Come on; be better than that.

Your competitors don't suck: Badmouthing others for your advantage is not the way. I've sold higher quality services against competitors who took short cuts and hid their flaws. I never bad mouthed them or 'anti sold' my competitors. Instead I always adopted the posture of educating my clients. I still do it.

If someone wants to ask me about another coach I'll give them guidance on how to assess their capabilities. And I can be humbly honest here, in my business there are some GREAT coaches and I am glad of the good they do – it reflects well on our industry.

If others are badmouthing you, or gossiping in any way, resist the urge to go that route. You'll win in the end.

"It is not the critic who counts; not the man who points out how the strong man stumbles, or where the doer of deeds could have done them better. The credit belongs to the man who is actually in the arena, whose face is marred by dust and sweat and blood; who strives valiantly; who errs, who comes short again and again, because there is no effort without error and shortcoming; but who does actually strive to do the deeds; who knows great enthusiasms, the great devotions; who spends himself in a worthy cause; who at the best knows in the end the triumph of high achievement, and who at the worst, if he fails, at least fails while daring greatly, so that his place shall never be with those cold and timid souls who neither know victory nor defeat."

Theodore Roosevelt

More Reading and Resources

We're getting to the end but there are a few more books I think you must read to prepare yourself for the world of entrepreneurship. Why? Because they've been so invaluable to me and I want to give you ALL I can. *I want you to WIN.* (Have I mentioned that already?)

The Four Agreements – it's a fable by Don Miguel Ruiz. You can read the entire book in an afternoon. The value of these four agreements is limitless and all the better in their simplicity. I could create a corporate culture with just this one book! In fact, I use it in EVERY client situation.
1. Be Impeccable With Your Word
2. Don't Take Anything Personally (this one is KILLER if you can achieve it)
3. Don't Make Assumptions
4. Always Do Your Best

The 15 Commitments of Conscious Leadership – This is a newer group, but their work is wonderfully powerful and exceptionally accessible.

Can you think in terms of living above the line or below the line? Above is open, curious and filled with possibility. Below the line is suspicious, closed and limited. They give you 15 clear commitments that you can adapt one at a time, practice them and gain strength and a personal process that works. Give them a read and you'll have a wealth of tools at your disposal. The context of their work will also help you keep the perspective that you can get what you want AND want what you get.

Getting Things Done – I don't know the numbers of sales, but this has to be the best and most popular book on time and project management of the last 18 years! David Allen has done an amazing job of giving simple rules, then building out the process through time saving apps, planners and other tools. The context of it is what really counts, and you can get the book or take a live seminar. I've done both and will again. Managing your time and being able to track your commitments without going crazy is a CORE REQUIREMENT of a successful solo-preneur or entrepreneur. DO NOT SKIP THIS BOOK!

Small Giants: Companies That Chose to be Great Instead of Big – Bo Burling ham wrote this back in 2007 and I read it then, plus his subsequent books. But this first book opened my eyes to what is possible in setting a vision for a company and has inspired millions since then. Great book for when you need some inspiration.

One More Tool – and it's a Power Tool

Mantras

Here's a short story. I was flying in to California to meet a fellow coach as we were delivering a training together. I arrived late evening and was hungry. It was colder than I expected, and I had a lot of prep work to complete before the next day. My colleague was waiting for me to have dinner with him and the restaurant would be closing soon.

The hotel said 'the shuttle will be there in 15 minutes'. They told me that again 25 minutes later and tried to tell that to me a third time 20 minutes later than that. At the end of my rope I was about to go all 'New Yorker' on the hotel clerk when I heard a voice in my head say, 'Everyone around me wins'. So, how could I make a win for this clerk and get what I needed?

'Ok', I said, 'Let me challenge you. I'm going to be the one person today you can tell the absolute truth to and I'll do my best to help you solve this problem. We both know this is a breakdown. How can we solve it so that you don't have to keep cringing every time I call you?'

The clerk asked me to hold, then called the shuttle driver on his personal cell. When he came back on the line with me he said that he had finally reached him and that there was an explanation – I didn't need it – and that he would guarantee the van would be there in under 10 minutes. It was there in five.

When I got checked in and ran over to the restaurant my partner laughed as I started to explain the situation. 'I heard the whole thing', he said, 'I just happened to be standing at the desk when you talked to the front desk clerk'. So, what?

Well, if I hadn't heard that voice in the back of my head, a fellow coach, a colleague I respect greatly, would have witnessed my 'New York' heat, and seen my dark side. Instead he heard me living up to that voice – my mantra. 'Everyone around me wins'.

Epilogue

I wrote this book from my coach's mantra: 'Everyone around me wins'. I go to work every day as a coach and I work hard to make sure that every day I move something or someone forward. I try to make each day count.

I also wrote this book from a very selfish perspective. I am tired of listening to people making excuses, blaming others, or otherwise lying to themselves or others.

If this book will help more people get to a place of 100% Responsibility, of living up to their word, of living in integrity, then my life will be improved. That's a selfish desire.

I will do my best to get the message of this book out with seminars, talks, articles, social media, and all the tools available to me, but I could use some help. I could use YOUR help.

If you want to help me change the world, then you have to share this book with people in your life. You have to tell them, if they find benefit, to share it with the people in their lives.

If we could all adapt the mindset of being the people responsible for making shit happen . . . Well you'd see progress like we haven't seen since Teddy Roosevelt lived from the mantra 'The buck stops here'.

Go out there and realize your dreams. It might be easy – maybe not. It might happen quickly or maybe it will take forever. Make it worth it. Make it count.

What you need to remember is this: if it is to be, it is up to YOU.

The choice is yours. Results? Or Excuses?

www.ingramcontent.com/pod-product-compliance
Lightning Source LLC
Chambersburg PA
CBHW020613220526
45463CB00006B/2579